Copyright © MCMLXXIV by
The C. R. Gibson Company, Norwalk, Connecticut
All rights reserved
Printed in the United States of America
Library of Congress Catalog Card Number: 72-92723
ISB: 0-8378-2006-5

Poems for Lovers

Written and compiled by
Basil Burwell

Photographs by
Edward H. Richardson III

Published by The C.R. Gibson Company
Norwalk, Connecticut

*Bend down and touch me with
your eyes
Make every morning hold a new
surprise.*

ROD McKUEN

*Before you kissed me only winds of heaven
  Had kissed me, and the tenderness of rain —
Now you have come, how can I care for kisses
  Like theirs again?*

SARAH TEASDALE

I do not know much about love,
    but I think that the rain
Caressed by the wind can tell me,
    or the blossoms blown
From the apple tree and
    swirling about my brain.
I do not know much, but there is
    something speaks in the bone,
Something quick as a star that
    falls at twelve,
Urgent as blood in the heart
    of a soaring bird.
I do not know much about love
    nor where to delve
In books for so large an answer,
    so great a word.
And what it is that wakes an
    ash to fire
I do not know; nor how the lazy tide
Becomes a beating wave,
    nor how I can inquire
But I think that the rain will speak
    when the wind has died,
And the bright voice in the bone
    will at last be clear
As the wave, as the fire, when you,
    sweet love, are near.

BASIL BURWELL

Come to me in the silence of the night;
Come in the speaking silence
of a dream
Come to me in dreams that I may live.

CHRISTINA ROSETTI

I heard a cry in the night,
    A thousand miles it came,
Sharp as a flash of light,
    My name, my name!

It was your voice I heard,
    You waked and loved me so —
I send you back this word,
    I know, I know!

SARAH TEASDALE

O my love
The pretty towns
All the blue tents of our nights together
And the lilies and the birds glad in our joy
The road through the forest
Where the surly wolf lived
And the snow at the top of the mountain
And the little
Rain falling on the roofs of the village
O my love my dear lady
The world is not very big
There is only room for our wonder
And the light leaning winds of heaven
Are not more sweet or pure
Than your mouth on my throat
O my love there are larks in our morning
And the finding flame of your hands
And the moss on the bank of the river
And the butterflies
And the whirling-mad
Butterflies!

KENNETH PATCHEN

Rapturous bridal! O wild heart,
To be part of thee, a part
Of this holy beauty here!
Sacred sorrow drawing near!
Sweet surrender! O my sweet,
Longingly my pulses beat!
Dappling thought, and fearful, of
The dear fury of thy love.

JOHN HALL WHEELOCK

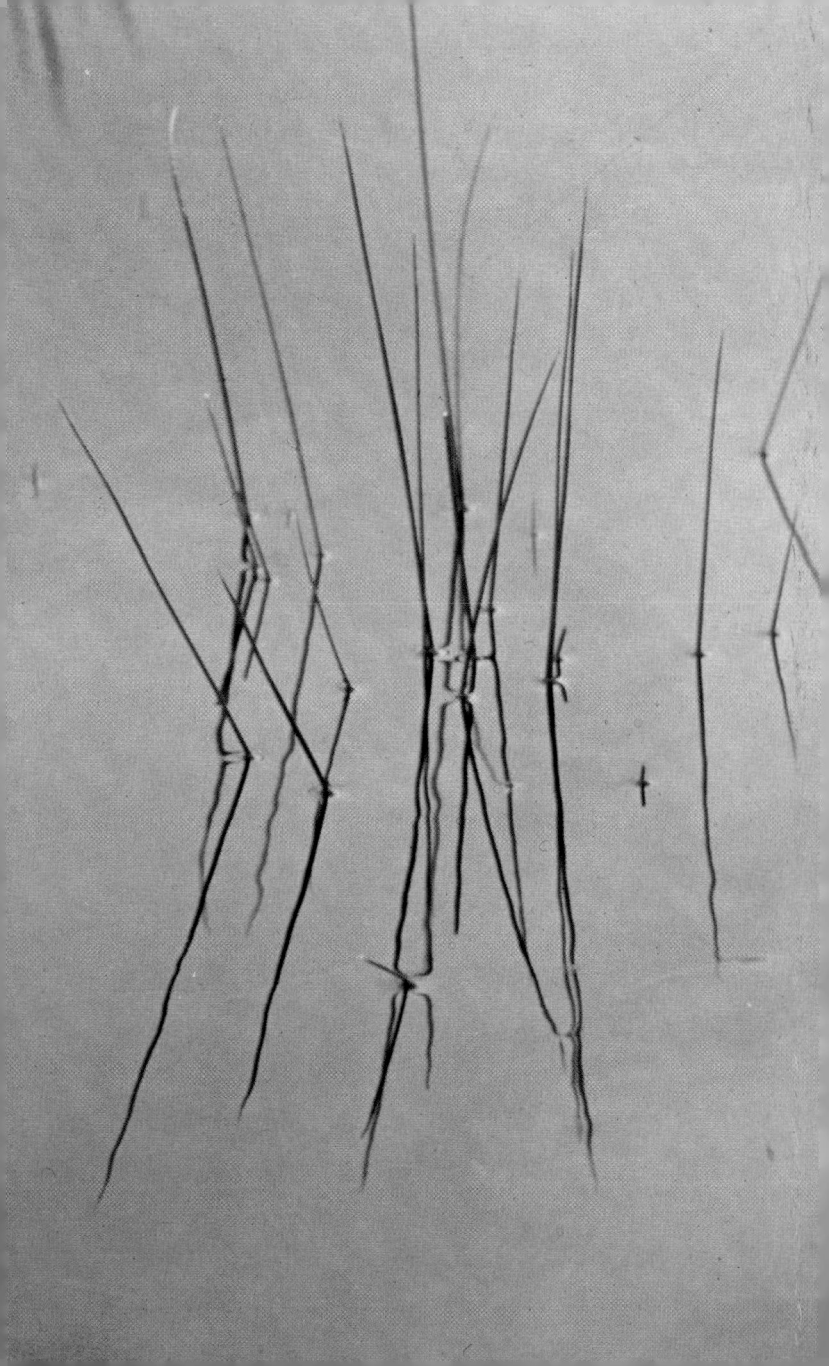

So let me be
Happy just to watch your smile
Oh, let me be
Resting here with you awhile
There is no need to
Feel you have to
Say a word to me.
This is the peace we want to last
    and last and last.

                           JERRY JEFF WALKER

Life goes slow without love.
It moves along unhurried.
The sun rises.

      The sun goes down.

                ROD McKUEN

How could I love you more?
I would give up
Even that beauty I have loved too well
That I might love you better.
Alas, how poor the gifts that
    lovers give —
I can but give you of my
    flesh and strength,
I can but give you these
    few passing days
And passionate words that since
    our speech began
All lovers whisper in all women's ears.

I try to think of some one gift
No lover yet in all the world
    has found;
I think: If the cold sombre gods
Were hot with love as I am
Could they not endow you with a star
And fix bright youth for ever
    in your limbs?
Could they not give you all things
    that I lack?

You should have loved a god;
    I am but dust.
Yet no god loved as loves this
    poor frail dust.

RICHARD ALDINGTON

When I go away from you
   The world beats dead
   Like a slackened drum.
   I call out for you against
      the jutted stars
   And shout into the ridges
      of the wind.

   AMY LOWELL

Stay near me. Speak my name.
   Oh, do not wander
By a thought's span, heart's impulse,
   from the light
We kindle here. You are my
   sole defender
(As I am yours) in this
   precipitous night,
Which over earth, till common
   landmarks alter,
Is falling, without stars,
   and bitter cold.
We two have but our burning selves
   for shelter.
Huddle against me. Give me your
   hand to hold.

   PHYLLIS McGINLEY

*ove, love! The night of golden nights is this,
Filled with the beating of all joyous wings;
For beauty is made holy in your kiss
And love and loveliness immortal things.
And all my being quivers with the cry
Of happy, happy, happy to the sky.*

EUNICE TIETJENS

*First, it was Joy
    that I was thinking of,
And when Joy came,
The face before me
    was so much like Love,
I thought the two the same;
I thought, also,
    the two in one enough,
Whatever the name,
For any man, to last
    a whole life through,
Call it Joy . . . or Love,
    I thought, or you . . . you.*

DAVID MORTON

Down the dripping pathway dancing through the rain,
Brown eyes of beauty, laugh to me again!

Eyes full of starlight, moist over fire,
Full of young wonder, touch my desire!

O like a brown bird, like a bird's flight,
Run through the rain drops lithely and light.

Body like a gypsy, like a wild queen,
Slim brown dress to slip through the green —

The little leaves hold you as soft as a child,
The little path loves you, the path that runs wild.

Who would not love you, seeing you move,
Warm-eyed and beautiful through the green grove?

Let the rain kiss you, trickle through your hair,
Laugh if my fingers mingle with it there,

Laugh if my cheek too is misty and drips —
Wetness is tender — laugh on my lips

The happy sweet laughter of love without pain,
Young love, the strong love, burning in the rain.

MAX EASTMAN

Love is not passion, love is not pride,
Love is a journeying side by side;
Not of the breezes, nor of the gale,
Love is the steady set of the sail.

ANONYMOUS

A sob of light from darkness, then the dawn,
And then the rumpled ruffling of the birds
The creaking house, the snow upon the lawn.
I drowse and sigh, remembering your words.
Then water cold upon the face to waken,
The toothbrush and the comb that stroke in time,
Fresh coffee in the pot, the eggs and bacon,
A thronging nonsense jostling the sublime.
And as I place the sticks upon the fire
I know a flame will burn forever on
The secret altar of my heart's desire
That never will be quenched and never gone
While you enkindle with that look . . . that look
I stand and dream and burn the eggs I cook.

BASIL BURWELL

There's something in the way she moves
Or looks my way or calls my name
That seems to leave this troubled
　　　world behind
And if I'm feeling down and blue
Or troubled by some foolish game
She always seems to make me change
　　　my mind

*And I feel fine any time she's around
    me now
She's around me now almost all the time
And if I'm well you can tell she's
    been with me now
She's been with me now quite a long
    long time
And I feel fine*

JAMES TAYLOR

Acknowledgments

The editor and the publisher have made every effort to trace the ownership of all copyrighted material and to secure permission from copyright holders of such material. In the event of any question arising as to the use of any material the publisher and editor, while expressing regret for inadvertent error, will be pleased to make the necessary corrections in future printings. Thanks are due to the following authors, publishers, publications and agents for permission to use the material indicated.

BIG BELLS INCORPORATED for selection from "Something In the Way She Moves" by James Taylor.

CHEVAL BOOKS, for selections from *In Someone's Shadow* by Rod McKuen.

COTILLION MUSIC, INC. for selection from "Please Let Me Be" by Jerry Jeff Walker, copyright © 1970 by Cotillion Music, Inc. and Danel Music, Inc.

MRS. MAX EASTMAN for "Rainy Song" from *Poems of Five Decades* by Max Eastman, copyright 1954 by Max Eastman.

HOUGHTON MIFFLIN COMPANY for selection from "Hippocrene" from *The Complete Works of Amy Lowell.*

ALFRED A. KNOPF, INC., for selection from "From the Mountains" from *Leaves in Windy Weather* by Eunice Tietjens, copyright 1929 by Alfred A. Knopf, Inc., renewed 1957 by Cloyd Head.

MACMILLAN PUBLISHING CO., INC., for two selections from *Collected Poems* by Sara Teasdale, copyright 1915 by Macmillan Publishing Co., Inc., renewed 1943 by Mamie T. Wheless.

NEW DIRECTIONS PUBLISHING CORP., for "Oh My Love the Pretty Towns" from *Collected Poems* by Kenneth Patchen. Copyright 1942 by Kenneth Patchen.

MRS. MARTHA RUTAN for "I Thought" by David Morton.

CHARLES SCRIBNER'S SONS for selection from "The Moonlight Sonata" by John Hall Wheelock from *Dust and Light*, copyright 1919 by Charles Scribner's Sons.

THE VIKING PRESS, INC., for selection from "Midcentury Love Letter" from *Times Three* by Phyllis McGinley, copyright 1953 by Phyllis McGinley. Originally appeared in The New Yorker.